DOWN
IN THE WOODS

Story and Pictures by Nicola Smee

"What's all this mess?" said Oliver's mother one morning.

The next morning there was even
more mess. "Please clean it up," his
mother said.

When he pulled the covers back to
make his bed, Oliver noticed leaves
in it—and mud on Bear's feet.
Oliver was puzzled.

Bear's up to something, thought
Oliver as he scrubbed him clean.
I'm going to keep an eye on him.

That night, when everyone was
supposed to be fast asleep, Oliver's
bear moved.

Oliver watched as he sneaked down the stairs.

He was just in time to see Bear
squeeze out through the cat door—
with a bag in his paw.

Down the garden path he went and
then...

he ran off through the trees.

I wonder what's in the bag,
Oliver thought to himself as he
followed Bear deep into the woods.

At last, in a clearing, Oliver saw
what his bear was up to!

I wish I could have joined in, he
thought as he made his way back home.

The next day Oliver hunted for anything
furry he could find.

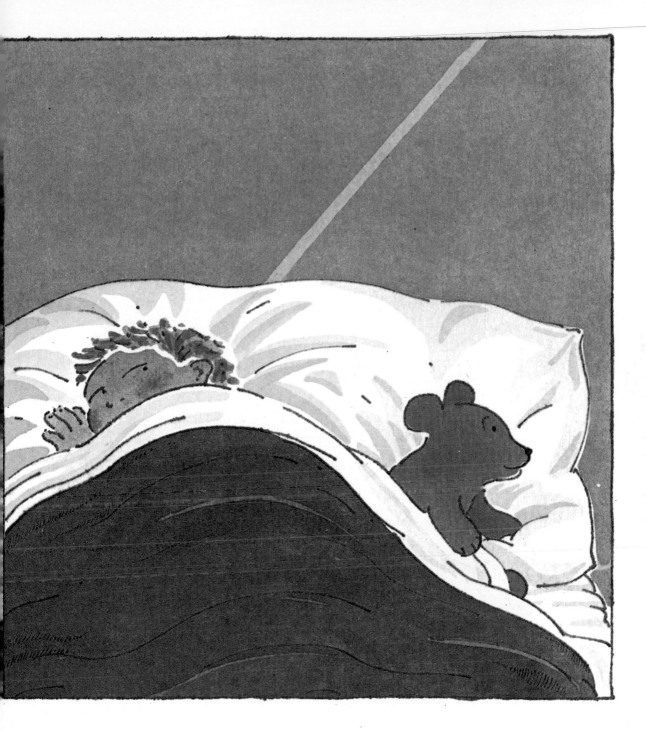

That evening he kept a watchful eye
on Bear. Sure enough, in the middle
of the night, Bear slipped quietly out
of bed. He was off again.

As Bear sneaked out, Oliver put on his
furry disguise, quickly blackened
his nose,

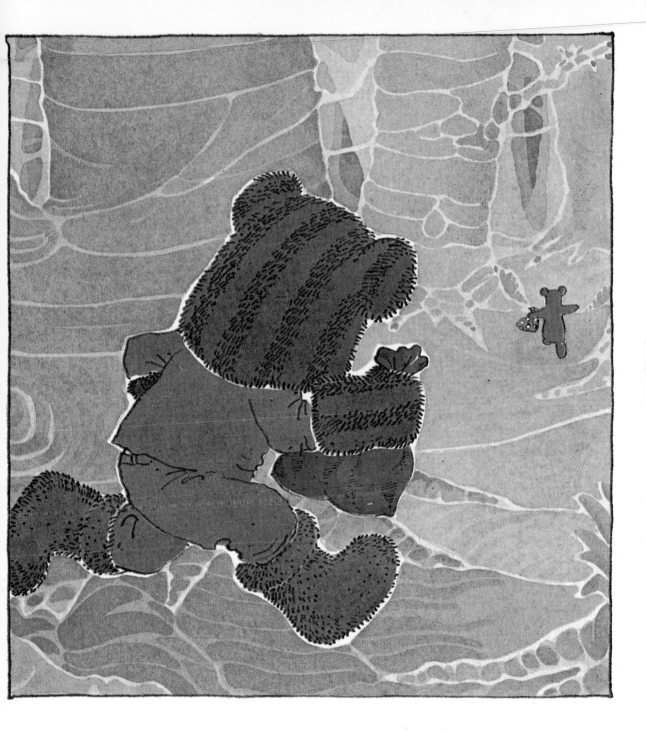

and rushed after him.

This time Bear arrived first and
Oliver watched as the other bears
appeared out of the trees.

Oliver felt shy but he came forward
and placed his bag on the tree trunk.

The bears seemed pleased to see a
new bear, especially one who brought
sweet rolls. Soon Oliver and the
bears were playing happily.

This is great, thought Oliver.

But suddenly a twig caught his furry
hat! The bears ran away frightened.
This new bear wasn't a bear at all!

"It's all right, he's my boy and he's
OK," shouted Oliver's bear to the
hiding bears.

Happy again, they all sat around the
tree trunk and ate their picnic.

On their way home Oliver's bear said
sleepily, "Will you come again? My
friends liked you."
"Yes, please," replied Oliver.

As they sneaked back up the stairs they
were careful to pick up any stray
leaves.

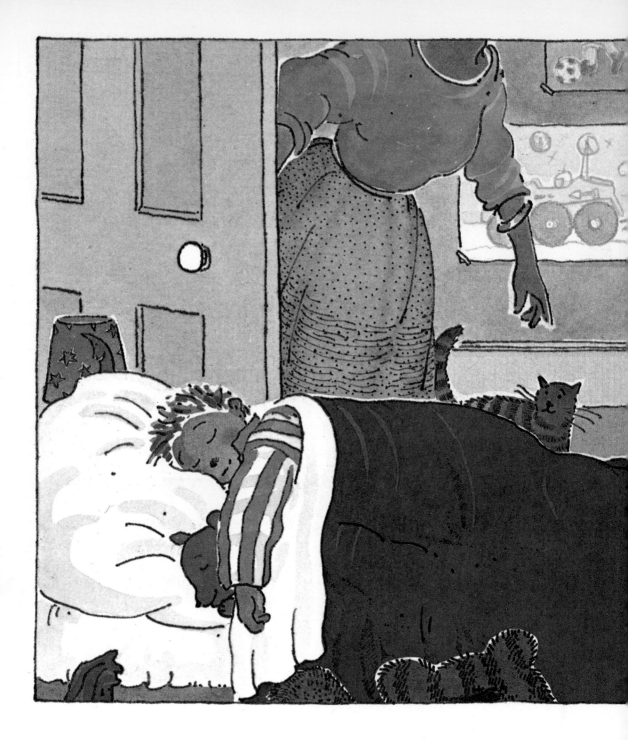

It was difficult to wake Oliver the
next morning.

"What's made you so sleepy?" his
mother asked.

"That's our little secret," whispered
Oliver to Bear.

This edition first published in the United States in 1989 by Gallery Books, an imprint of W.H. Smith Publishers, Inc.,
112 Madison Avenue, New York, New York 10016. Produced for Gallery Books by Joshua Morris Publishing, Inc. in
association with William Collins Sons & Co. Ltd. Text and illustrations copyright © 1985 by Nicola Smee. All rights reserved.
ISBN 0-8317-4421-9 Printed in Hong Kong.